Belly Dance Business

101

The Beginners Guide to Being a Professional Belly Dancer

By
Helen Blondel

Acknowledgements

I would like to thank

My mother, Sandra Blondel, for being my biggest support system throughout my life, artistic journey, and career.

My father, Rupert Blondel, for teaching me the importance of value and work ethic that I take with me in every endeavor I pursue. Rest in paradise.

Contents

Introduction

If there is one thing, I learned from being a professional entertainer for almost two decades, it's that figuring your way around making it a career path can be a major challenge. This is especially true when you're just starting out. Being a singer years before discovering belly dance, I was no stranger to the stage. However, when I embarked on my journey as a belly dancer 16 years ago, I never thought it would lead me to where I am today. Becoming a professional, appearing on TV, performing in shows, and hosting my own classes seemed like a distant dream. However, the dream was there, and every dream is accompanied by challenges to overcome.

After years of practice and improving my craft, the new challenge I faced was being able to turn this passion into a profitable career. After all, I had the talent. I remember times I'd go out with my friends for a stroll along the Miami nightlife scene, and sometimes I'd come across Mediterranean restaurants. There would almost always be a belly dancer performing her heart out in a beautiful costume, delighting the patrons and creating an enchanting atmosphere. I'd watch in admiration, but deep-down wonder, "How can that be me?"

Throughout my many academic endeavors in high school and university, friendships, relationships, and other trials & tribulations, one thing always remained a constant in my life—my passion for Oriental Dance. Passion was a big factor in creating a career out of performing. It has kept me going throughout multiple rejections. I recall asking experienced dancers for opportunities and either being left on "seen" or given vague answers like "just keep working hard." When going to direct sources, like restaurant venues, I'd often be welcomed with a big fat "No" before even getting to showcase my skills. It was frustrating and even discouraging at times. If it weren't for passion, I think I wouldn't have had the tenacity to keep pursuing this dream.

After years of continuing my involvement in this beautiful art form, I've met some amazing dancers, gained extensive experience, and learned so much about what it takes to progress professionally as a belly dancer. Making a career out of Oriental dance is not just a one-step action and I only learned this over years of trial-and-error. In this book, I aim to share with you the many things I learned so that you can have clarity on your unique path as a professional.

Identify Your Purpose

Before taking any further steps to move forward as a working belly dancer, it's important to first identify *why* you want to be a professional. As with any profitable career path, it is still a job with which you will identify. For this reason, you must understand your purpose.

During a casual conversation about my desire to take performing to the next level, a successful dancer and mentor of mine advised that to truly be considered a professional belly dancer, I must first find out "who I am." Upon hearing this, I had no idea what she meant. I knew I loved dancing and was good at it. What more could there be to it? It was a profound question that I wasn't prepared for. For the next several months I pondered over this *"who I am"* question, and finally figured it out. Who you are is your overall essence as a dancer, and aligns with your purpose.

Of the many steps I go over in this guide, this one may be the hardest to grasp because of its uniqueness to each individual. Identifying your purpose is an internal question and no one can answer it for you other than yourself. All of us have different reasons as to why we dance. For some, the purpose might be to positively impact others' lives through teaching. For others, it may be to acquire fame. Some dancers' purpose could even be to share something more meaningful with their audience.

Given that your intentions of pursuing a career in Oriental Dance are genuine, there is no wrong answer. I can't stress enough how much finding your purpose as an artist is not a one size fits all action. Some dancers might be able to realize this in a matter of minutes, for others it may take months. It is important to be patient with yourself and highly introspective, as well. Knowing your purpose as a dancer will determine how you move forward in this career path. You may also find as you blossom in your professional endeavors, your purpose or identity as a dancer may change down the line. This is okay and honestly quite common in the cycle of an artist.

Identify Your Primary Clientele

A mistake many of us artists (myself included) make is that we focus solely on our art and lose sight of the business aspect of what we do. When transitioning from a student dancer to making a profit from your craft, you are no longer *just* an artist. You are a businessperson and must answer questions key to its success. One of these is the main demographic you plan to market to.

If you've already identified your purpose and who you are as a dancer, this step may be slightly easier for you. When you know what your goals are, you will be able to filter out any type of client that doesn't align with that.

Will you cater to upscale private events or do you prefer restaurants? Do you wish to perform for a certain age group, gender, or other demographic of people? Maybe you prefer to dance for & teach other dancers rather than entertain a general audience. These questions within a question may seem tedious, but I've learned that it is a beneficial step in creating your business plan. Once you determine who exactly you are marketing to, this will set the path for everything else in your career.

When I first started doing belly dance gigs, I didn't really have a primary clientele in mind. All I knew were two things—I wanted to get paid and I wanted to get my name out there, leading to more opportunities to get paid! This is a valid mindset and I know many dancers who just start out thinking this way. Some performers just dance any and everywhere with extraordinarily little thought and end up making a lot of money. However, I've noticed that once I started marketing to a specific demographic of clients, not only did my business plan improve, but so did the quality and pay of my gigs.

If you are very green in the industry, you might be eager to start, no matter what kind of gig it is. You may just want to hop on the opportunity to finally dance and make a profit. This is okay but consider doing this with a purpose.

As I was doing my first shows I used to think that all gig-types were one-size-fits-all. After my first dozen events/restaurant appearances, it didn't take long for me to realize this couldn't be farther from the truth. I quickly discovered my preferred clientele.

Use your first few gigs for trial and error. See what type of events and demographic you like performing for (it will be different for everyone). You will soon notice a pattern of what you do and don't like, and will be able to go from there.

In my experience, I've been better off with one focus. By honing in on a specific audience, I was able to get notoriety within their network, as well as given the opportunity to expand to other niches as well.

Identify Your Dance Style

Much like a target clientele, it's important to have a specific style that makes you unique. You've most likely studied belly dance for a significant enough amount of time for you to know what your style is. However, if not, this is something worth looking into for a key reason: attracting your desired audience.

Your dance style is closely associated with the type of client you prefer to attract because certain demographics tend to like certain styles. Certain events may call for a dancer whose technique is flowy and elegant, while others would prefer one who is more earthy and understated. Music and costuming are also aspects that one must take into consideration. The music and outfit of choice at a Middle Eastern wedding would differ greatly from that of a hookah bar at night, for example. Therefore, it's important to ask yourself the following,

- What style(s) of music do I enjoy the most?

- What are my favorite costumes to wear? Is there anything I *won't* wear?

- What characterizes my dance technique and are there things I can improve on to better suit my target audience?

If you haven't already, you may find it easier to discover your primary clientele based on your answers to these questions. Asking yourself these things will make you more self-aware as a dancer.

But what about if you don't have a preferred style of music or costuming, or what if you're not sure how to pinpoint your technique? A great way to discover these preferences is to expose yourself to all that the Oriental Dance community has to offer. You can do this by attending dance festivals. There, you can take workshops of world-renowned master instructors and see what you like and don't like while simultaneously learning new techniques. Another perk to belly dance festivals is their gala shows, where you can watch many seasoned professionals perform various styles. You can then assess what performances you enjoyed the most and see if there were any consistencies with what attracted your attention.

If attending an Oriental dance convention is not possible at the moment, the internet is a powerful tool! You can go to belly dance pages on platforms, such as Instagram, and study the many different dancers' performances. After identifying what you like, the most important thing is to then put this into practice by rehearsing and investing in costumes that align with your unique style.

Image

Once you decide to become a professional dancer, you are now a business,
and performing is your service. Every
successful product on the market has a
brand. In this case, since the product/ser-
vice is your dancing, your image is your
brand.

In business, branding is defined as any
feature that identifies one seller's good or
service as distinct from those of other sellers.
Think about it even outside of the dance

realm. From your favorite musical artist to your favorite beverage. All of these companies have a logo, color, or general feel image-wise, where one would easily be able to distinguish them from a competitor company. Successful businesses have good branding.

Being in decent physical shape is important in this profession. However, a common misconception around belly dancers (and performance artists collectively, for that matter) is that one must look like a fitness model to be successful and get work. This isn't necessarily the case. I've seen dancers gain notoriety, not because they were pretty or had a certain body type, but because they had a unique look—in other words, a brand. So, the next question to ask yourself is, what sets *you* apart from the rest?

The concept of finding your image is similar to that of identifying your dance style mentioned in the previous chapter. However, your image holds a distinctive weight because it is the first thing people see before they even get to witness your dance.

Now more than ever, the supply of belly dancers is heavily saturated. This is especially true if you live in a metropolitan area. Having the typical cookie-cutter image may work in some cases. However, in a market with so much competition, possessing an image that distinguishes you from the "dime-a-dozen" instantly sets you apart. You become more *recognizable*. This naturally increases the probability of being booked, or, at the very least considered for booking.

An example of a belly dancer who brands herself exceptionally, is world-renowned dancer, Oxana Bazaeva. She is notorious for her curly, bright red hair and eccentric body-hugging costumes. Her image is often imitated, but these dancers are almost always called out for taking inspiration from Oxana's "staple" look.

Keep this in mind when finding the visual aspects that set you apart. Some people may have physical attributes that are naturally unique, making it easier to identify their image. For others, it may be something as specific as a costume piece that they, and only they, are notorious for wearing. As with any other successful business, developing your image often takes time and that's okay! This is your chance to be creative.

Get Your Foot in the Door

For most newly professional entertainers, getting work is the biggest hurdle to overcome. After all, the purpose of this guide is to assist in navigating your career as a belly dancer. Therefore, gigs are the most important part! But let me be clear when I say, rejection is a norm, and having the drive to move past that is imperative.

When I was just beginning, the process of getting booked was so frustrating. I faced a lot of rejection when trying to get my foot in the door. The market was starting to become saturated at that time and venues already had their preferred dancers. I had little to no reputation in comparison to other entertainers with a strong network. After copious attempts at trying the same thing and constantly getting "don't call us, we'll call you" replies and ignored emails in return, I eventually became exhausted. There was a period I stopped trying, but not for long.

My love for this art form was too strong and I soon found myself immersed in various activities and events that led me to where I am now as I write this. I took a completely different route than the first time. After all, the definition of insanity is doing something repeatedly and expecting different results. In this chapter, I'll be sharing the various actions I took that helped me greatly in not only getting work but also meeting amazing people in the community and learning a lot.

It's important to realize that each artist has their own path. What worked for me might not work for another dancer. However, here are the following steps one can take to highly increase the probability of getting booked based on my experience.

Become an Active Member of a Dance Company

As mentioned before, the moment you decide to make a profit from your craft, you are now a business. In any business, having a network is key to its success (keep in mind, most of the steps I go over in this chapter are somehow linked to networking) and with dance, there is no exception.

Aside from possible gig opportunities, joining a dance company has additional benefits. Regardless of how good you are, there is *always* something to learn along the way. Sometimes as soloists, we can get so consumed in doing moves or interpreting music our own way, we run the risk of being one-dimensional. In a group setting with a director calling the creative shots, you are suddenly exposed to a new way of doing things. When practicing next to ten other people, it's easier to see the differences (yours and theirs, too) and gain new perspectives on what you could add to your solo dance!

Joining a professional troupe tests your resilience, character, and professionalism. In my singing and dancing career combined, I've been in several performance groups. While each is quite different, these three facts remain true for all. In a dance company, it is no longer just about *you*. It is about your equal contribution to the collective. There will be days you are expected to attend rehearsals when you simply don't want to or moments where the director might seem strict and truly test your patience. And, let's face it—long hours in a studio full of dancers with contrasting personalities is a challenge in and of itself! However, in my experience, enduring the realities of working in a team ultimately changed me for the better.

One becomes well-rounded and exposed to what it's like to work under pressure. Therefore, how you rise above these challenges is critical. This is your chance to prove yourself, not only to your director but also to the studio owner. Both likely have a solid network of clients they work with and hard work rarely goes unnoticed. Being an A-player in a dance troupe is a great way to exhibit professionalism and drive, making you more likely to be the one they contact to fill a booking.

Join a Talent Agency

Much like dance companies, most talent agencies require an audition and/ or track record of professionalism to get in. However, they are different in that they focus more on booking the solo artist at gigs for a percentage of the profit. Agencies are a good option for dancers with a little-to-no network. Since booking talent is their primary revenue source, agencies have their own pool of clients and constantly make sales efforts to grow this clientele (this translates to more gig opportunities for you)!

There are different types of talent firms out there and none of them are quite equal. Some agencies exclusively offer dance entertainment ranging from ballet, belly dance, jazz, etc. Certain talent firms offer limitless types of variety-acts (emcee, promo modeling, singing, dance, etc.). Contrastingly, there are even agencies that specialize mainly in Belly Dance entertainment. In fact, some belly dance studios with professional dance companies simultaneously run these types of agencies, as well. When looking for talent firms to join, make sure to do your research.

A major pro to joining any of these agency-types is that the guesswork is done for you. In addition to finding clientele, they handle the other administrative duties such as phone & email correspondence, performers' insurance coverage, and money handling. However, one must consider the possible downsides, too, and how to better make a prepared decision:

- Most reputable entertainment firms require you to sign a contract. It's okay to read the agreement twice and take it home if you have to before signing it. Some companies have strict non-compete clauses and others don't have one at all.

- It is normal for agencies to take a percentage of what you make per gig. This is called a *booking fee or agency fee*. Some agencies' booking fees are higher than others, so it's important to assess the amount you're comfortable with. Find out the average booking fee of agencies in your area. A larger than average agency fee *could* be a possible red flag.

- When in doubt, do your research. There are scam companies masked as talent agencies that prey on artists seeking work. There are also legitimate entertainment agencies that simply have a poor track record of finding work for their talent, or even paying them! The internet is a useful tool and so is word of mouth. Be wary if a company has constant negative reviews.

- It's okay to walk away from an opportunity if something doesn't feel right. As professionals, we are sometimes led to make hard decisions to protect our business.

- I've seen talent firm scams and have also witnessed poorly run entertainment companies. However,

I've also been involved with several legitimate talent agencies that led to many awesome opportunities. It's all about staying informed, avoiding illegitimate businesses, and finding the right reputable agency for you. If you live in a metropolitan area, there's likely several!

Join an Entertainment Services Booking Platform

Upon discovering my dad was terminally ill, I didn't think twice to leave everything behind and be with him during his final days in my hometown. That also meant leaving behind my belly dance troupe and talent agency, as well.

Although I had a strong network in the city I built my profession in, the town I would soon transition to was a different story. I moved to my hometown knowing almost no one in the belly dance community. At the time there was no belly dance agency I knew of in the area and I had no idea where or how to get work. I felt like a beginner all over again. That was until I had a pivotal phone call with a belly dance instructor to whom I look up to this day. She suggested I make a profile on an event services site.

Platforms, such as GigSalad and The Bash (formerly known as Gigmasters) are internet marketplaces that connect performers of all kinds with everyday people seeking entertainment for their events. Up until that conversation with my instructor, I had no inkling that something like this existed! Although I'm sure there are dozens of these types of platforms on the web, I registered for the two I previously mentioned. The results were wonderful. Through these sites I got booked for numerous events, leading to me growing my client network, reputation, exposure to other dancers in the community, and eventually independent bookings outside of the website.

Joining an entertainment services platform gives you more autonomy than talent agencies or dance studio opportunities in that you have direct and independent communication with your lead from start to finish. You make your own profile with photos and videos, can set up your description however you see fit, and have control of your location preferences. When an event planner needs a specific type of entertainer for an event, they can send out a general inquiry that notifies all entertainers of that variety in the area. They also have the option to sift through the many artist profiles and contact the entertainer they want directly. The talent would then either have the choice of responding with their compensation requirements based on the details provided or rejecting the gig. After that, it's ultimately up to the planner to confirm the booking.

Much like talent agencies, however, these websites also take a percentage of what you make as a booking fee. In addition to the booking fee, a paid membership is also required to have an active profile on the platform. This is something one should think about when considering this option. Joining the aforementioned websites jump-started my ability to get profitable work as a belly dancer in a town where it would've otherwise taken a lot more time and investment to do so.

Set Your Price

Determining the value of your entertainment services when you're just starting can be an intimidating process. When I commenced my belly dance career, I was in constant conflict with myself regarding price. I didn't want to set my rate too high because I had little gigging experience and was hungry for work. However, I also didn't want to set my price too low, because then I wouldn't profit! After years of involvement with the belly dance community, gigging experience, and exposure to the entertainment industry as a whole, I've learned important factors regarding setting your price that must be taken into account.

Know the Average Dancer Rate in Your Area—and Avoid Undercutting

Undercutting, or offering services at a lower price than competitors with the intent of snagging the gig, is a big problem in the belly dance industry because it devalues us in the eyes of the everyday person. When a dancer offers their performances to a restaurant or event planner for extremely low rates (or sometimes even free in exchange for exposure), it teaches these people to expect less. Think of the popular saying, '*why buy the cow when you can get the milk for free?*' From a buyer's perspective, it makes little sense to pay hundreds of dollars on an entertainer when less-experienced dancers are willing to perform for free or half the price. Truth is, Oriental dance artists who are serious about their craft spend thousands of dollars in their lifetime on professional costumes, stage grade makeup, and dance lessons, not to mention years of hard work to get to where they are today. Sadly, undercutting cannot be completely eliminated from our industry, but by pricing your rates within the average range of your competitors, you will contribute to re-teaching the everyday person to respect this art form and value it.

Finding out the industry standard is relatively easy. However, each city may vary slightly in average rates based on dancer supply and demand. For example, the average rate of a 30-minute belly dance show in Orlando, FL would probably differ from that of a show in Manhattan, NY. Most metropolitan areas have private Facebook groups with names such as *Belly Dancers of [Insert Metro Here]* that you can join. See what other dancers in your area are charging by either going to their website or asking them directly. Since undercutting is a pervasive problem in our industry, the belly dance community is vocal about standard prices and sharing what they can if it means prevention of such lowballing.

Know Your Worth

Once you are familiar with the standard price range in your city, it's now time to assess where you want to be on that scale based on your skills and experience. When I first began, my rate was on the lower end of that spectrum and now it is on the higher end. After gaining experience, improving my craft, and getting more booking requests, I knew when it was time to increase my rates.

Determining the starting rates for your shows is a personal decision. Regardless of how low or high it is, as long as it is within the average rate of other professional belly dancers, it is a valued price.

Communicating your rate to clients can also be an intimidating process, especially if you're new and want nothing more than to be booked and gain that experience. When a potential client requests your rates to perform, it may be tempting to lower your price "just this one time" for the sake of "getting chosen" as the one to be booked. This is an understandable mindset to have, but also detrimental to your short-term profit and your long-term *perceived value*. The mindset of thinking that gigs choose us puts us in a vulnerable spot as artists (which is exactly what cheap clients want). However, the moment we switch to a "We choose the gigs" mindset, we reclaim our power as performers and only value the clients who value us (trust me, there are many clients who do)! By stating your non-discounted rate to a lead, you place the ball in their court to either show value to your art by accepting your price or exhibit that they aren't worth your time as a client in the first place.

Negotiation is another situation one may often encounter in their career as a belly dancer. Once you mention your rate, a lead may ask if you can go any lower for various reasons. While a potential client trying to negotiate a lower rate for our hard work can be annoying, I use this opportunity to create a perceived value for them. Potential clients are often just everyday people looking to save money while bringing entertainment to their guests. By answering their inquiries in a patient and informative way, we can educate them on our value as an individual dancer. Here are examples of generic responses to some of the most popular client-attempts to negotiate:

"But I know a dancer who charges less."

My Response: The rate I charge reflects my experience, years of training, and investment in quality attire, makeup, and props. You may find cheaper options out there, but similar quality is not guaranteed, and most dancers with similar experience charge a similar amount. For this reason, my rate is firm. If you would like to move forward in booking me at my rate, I'd be glad to perform. If not, I understand and wish you luck in your search.

"I can't offer pay, but I promise that my event is high profile and you will gain lots of exposure and/or great tips."

My Response: This is my profession and the amount I charge for my services is $[insert rate here]. Should anything change and you are able to compensate me at that rate, feel free to contact me.

"My budget is $[insert lower price here]. Is there any way you can fit into my budget?"

My Response: I understand your budget is $[insert lower price here]. However, I am unable to lower my rate. As a business, it would be unethical to charge less to one person for the same service that I've charged many others a higher price for. For this reason and to maintain the integrity of my business, my rate is firm across the board. Should your budget change and you'd like to book my services, feel free to contact me.

"No thank you, that is too expensive."

My Response: I understand your concern with my rate. Good luck with your search and should anything change, feel free to contact me.

While each response is slightly different depending on the question, the general feel of the replies remains the same. As you can see, these responses are concise, show empathy to the lead's situation, leave the ball in their court, and most importantly, they show that you are not afraid to walk away. In any business deal, the entity that gets the shorter end of the stick is the often one who was afraid to walk away during negotiation.

When one is comfortable with leaving despite an offer being set on the table, it shows the offeror two things—that this person has other options and that they won't settle for less, both of which increase the offeree's perceived value. High value products attract high value customers. This also applies to artists and their entertainment services. By responding to undervaluing inquiries with class, understanding, and freedom of outcome, you exemplify yourself as a high value belly dance artist and businessperson. It is important to know your worth and express it professionally. There will be many clients who won't see value in booking you regardless of what you do. Let go of this type of client and focus on the clients who see your worth.

Online Presence

Now more than ever, social media and the internet as a whole are a critical tool for the success of any business. Decades ago, customers would head to the yellow pages or word of mouth when they needed a professional service. Now, everything from company information to client reviews is one click away! For this reason, having a strong online presence is incredibly important. The great thing about creating your online presence is that as useful as it is to yourself and potential clients, it costs very little (and sometimes nothing at all) to do so. The two most powerful ways I was able to transform my online presence and increase my opportunities exponentially was with my website and social media use. Many dancers use one or the other. I've seen dancers with incredible social media but no website, vice versa. However, I've seen the best results when combining both.

Website

A good basic website for any performer should include the following: A bio & credentials, quality photos, credentials, rates, and a contact page.

Every dancer has a different story that makes them unique. Your bio, or 'about me' section, is the perfect place to spotlight this information. When leads access your website, they want to know who you are and your background as a performer. This includes your credentials such as special awards, years of experience, specialties, or anything other accomplishments that set you apart from other dancers in your area.

As mentioned earlier, the market for dancers in most metropolitan areas is saturated. Competition is inevitable. If someone is on your website looking to fill a gig for an event, they are most likely looking at the websites of at least two other entertainers! Now more than ever, customers are becoming more aware of their spending and want the most value for their dollar. Use your 'About me' section as a way to market your skills and why you are the best option to be hired. Were you ever on TV? List that. Do you dance with special props? List all of the ones you are familiar with. Did you win a competition? Regardless of how long ago it was, it still counts as an award and should be recognized. If you are just starting out on the professional side of performing, you might not have credentials like these. Make sure to emphasize your passion for dance in your bio! Any other milestones, such as the pro dancer(s) you've studied under or any festival workshops you've attended count, too.

Good quality photos are imperative to your website. While many potential clients will focus on the entertainer's skill based on their bio, others care more about the visual. Therefore, it's important for your website to reflect the full package. Photos represent one's image, so make sure to have professional shots that reflect your unique brand as a dancer.

I currently list starting rates on my website. Contrarily, some professional belly dancers do not list their rates on their websites. The school of thought for performers who don't list their price is that:

- Other professionals will see their rates and undercut accordingly.

- Their rates vary depending on the type of event, location, duration, etc.

- They do not want to scare off customers with the high prices, so they'd rather just get serious inquiries where they can then disclose the rate.

I understand these concerns. When one is choosing to go professional, they should select the option ideal for them. You might find it best for you to omit rates from your website, as well. However, here are the benefits I've found in total transparency of rates on my website:

- Time is of the essence for potential clients. By listing your services and corresponding prices on the website, you take away the guesswork of them having to reach out to you just for a price inquiry (and their possible embarrassment if they can't afford your rate).

- You set the expectations so there are no surprises. Once your rates for each service and any upcharges for mileage, etc. are live for anyone to see on your website, customers are made aware of all this information before contacting you. If they question your rate or upcharges, you can simply direct them to the 'services' section of your page for reference.

- Other dancers *may* use your rates for influence, but this can also be a good thing. It is natural for businesses of any kind to want to see what their competitors are doing. As discussed in the previous chapter, some dancers simply don't know what to charge. When they see other dancers in the community charging within the standard rate of their area, they will be likely to charge the same, which actually prevents what I call 'accidental undercutting,' or charging less because one simply doesn't know the higher running rate.

Your 'Contact' page is a great gateway to sealing the deal for a possible gig. An artist can have an exceptional bio, photo gallery, and rates page, but if there is no place to contact you, clients will get discouraged. Remember, time is of the essence for potential customers and there are other options! You've worked so hard to make a great website, so make sure your contact info is visible with options, too. Most website hosts will give the option for you to add a contact box requiring the site visitor's name, email, phone number, and inquiry. I also highly recommend leaving links to your social media, business email, and business phone number, somewhere on the page as well. This gives your lead several different ways to reach you, making it more convenient for them. Convenience for a prospective client often leads to conversion to an actual customer.

Social Media

In this day and age, checking social media is a part of almost everyone's daily routine. Therefore, utilizing platforms like Instagram, TikTok, Facebook, Youtube, and similar sites is a great way to build a fanbase and gain exposure to potential clients.

Content is key. Make valuable content related to your art, tweaking it to each platform. What works on Youtube, such as a full performance with a description, won't work as well on Instagram on TikTok which generally favors shorter videos. Taking the time to create content designated for each platform will work wonders and allow you to gain followers rapidly.

Use hashtags. On Instagram, use hashtags such as #bellydance, #bellydancer,

#orientaldance, and up to 30 hashtags that you feel are relevant to your post. That, as well as using general location in your posts, will influence the algorithm to suggest your content to people in your area and those with a history of interest in one of your hashtags. This will increase your probability of attracting a relevant following which could lead to gaining clientele down the line.

Consistency is also key. From my experience, four to seven posts a week are ideal. However, if that is too much, try to post at least twice a week. The more times you put your content out there for others to see, the more exposure you will have to a higher amount of people. In addition to attracting new followers, consistent content will also remind your current fanbase of why they followed you in the first place. For those specifically in your area, this is important because the more they see your content, the more likely they will be to have you in mind when planning an event that requires belly dance entertainment.

As previously mentioned, make sure your image is reflected consistently on your social media and posts. This is not only what will draw people in, but it's also what will make you memorable.

Professionalism

You may have gotten the gig, a decent follower base, and things are looking up for you as a professional entertainer. This is amazing because all of these steps take incredibly hard work. However, the key to *retaining* clients is your professionalism. This is true even outside of the entertainment industry. Let's take the food & beverage industry, for example. A restaurant may have memorable commercials, competitive prices, and delicious food—but if the staff is unprofessional, would you go there again? Probably not. Any company that seeks to be in business for a long time must think of their *customer retention*, which is just as important as gaining new customers.

The same holidays occur every twelve months, meaning each year the same holiday parties are bound to happen. Being professional and providing quality entertainment to your client increases a client's chance of booking you the following years to come. This also increases the probability of positive *word of mouth* marketing to their friends and family about you. This, paired with the first-time clients you receive, will lead to way more long-term revenue than if you just had one-time clients alone.

Professionalism is such an important step when deciding to make a career in belly dance, that I've divided it up into two main parts—Communication and Action.

Professional Communication

Quick Correspondence

The early bird gets the worm, and this is also true for business. Think about it from the client's point of view. Your potential customer is stressed because they are planning an event. They probably have a budget they can't exceed and most likely other factors of the event they are also responsible for. I can't stress enough how much time is of the essence! If a lead contacts you, you can almost be sure they are contacting other belly dancers in your area. The sooner you respond, the higher possibility you have of actually getting booked. If you promise on your website to return inquiries within 72 hours, make sure to follow through! This is also true for direct messages on social media. Respond as soon as you can.

Direct Communication to Phone Calls If Possible

Emails are great, but in my experience, there is nothing like one-on-one verbal communication. I also find that one is able to acquire more information in far less time via. phone call rather than an email or text message. Instead of spending up to two days of back-and-forth conversations via. email, your lead can get all their questions answered in minutes during one simple call. This will also give you the opportunity to inquire what they are looking for, assess whether you are the right fit for the gig, and not waste more time than needed if you aren't.

It's also important to respect privacy, as well. If a lead first contacts you by email or text message, it may be wise not to immediately call them. Instead, respond saying you'd love to discuss their inquiry with them over the phone, asking when they'd be available for a phone call.

When in Doubt, Communicate Formally

This should go without saying, but the way you handle yourself verbally says a lot about you to your potential customer. Some clients will be quite informal with you and that's ok. You don't have to speak like a customer service representative at all times, but there is a line that generally shouldn't be crossed. Even if a client uses profanity with you in conversation (assuming you are both laid back and comfortable with this), it is in your best interest not to reciprocate those profane words. You are a business and should represent yourself as such.

Kindness Goes a Long Way

There will be times that a lead or current customer will do or say something that you don't like. A common example would be like the one mentioned in Chapter 6 with a potential client trying to haggle you down on a price. Your immediate feelings may be that the lead is undervaluing you or disrespecting you by asking a lower price. However, just as exemplified in the aforementioned chapter, don't let your personal feelings set the tone for your response. Instead, just handle the conversation with class. If there is ever a time where a person is persistent with the matter even after you respond professionally, you are able to block them. This is a better option than responding in a rude manner which ultimately just lowers your brand.

Professional Actions

Be Punctual

In the typical 9-5 office job, one is expected to show up on time. With the exception of a first offense or emergency, there are serious consequences of showing up late to work. Not being on time reflects a lack of discipline and disinterest in your work, reflecting poor professionalism. This principle is no different when it comes to being an entertainer.

Customers pay you for your services with the expectation that you will show up to their event on time. The standard is to meet that expectation.

Of course, there are many situations that could lead to being late, such as extensive makeup preparation, a costume malfunction, traffic, or getting lost on your way to the location. When preparing for your event, it's important to take all this into consideration when getting ready. If you would normally take an hour to get ready, allow yourself at least 90 minutes to do so. If the GPS says that your gig is 30 minutes away, start heading there 45 – 60 minutes ahead of time to leave room for if you get lost or unexpected traffic. Worst-case scenario, you will get there early and have nothing to do for a few minutes. Best case scenario, you will have spared yourself time and your reputation by still being punctual to your event. Trust me, being over-prepared is much better than being underprepared and running the risk of a client's dissatisfaction in your service.

Walk Away

I mentioned before that when faced with online harassment, it's better to block them than to further engage with them down that road. However, what if you're faced with hostility in person? The same principle applies to when with a current customer, lead, or even fellow dancer is conducting themselves unprofessionally with you. A plethora of situations can occur at events where you are dancing, especially when there is alcohol involved. We are all human and things like a rude comment from a patron or dance colleague can easily facilitate a confrontational response from you. Remember that conflict is not worth you lowering your brand and reputation. A quote I live by (or at least try to live by) is, "If it won't affect you in 5 years, don't let it bother you for more than 5 minutes." This is otherwise known as the *5-by-5 rule.* In those initial 5 minutes, use that time to walk away from the situation. The main exception is when you feel threatened and/ or feel like you are in danger. Safety should always be kept in mind.

Administrative Planning

A big mistake that I made when starting out as a professional belly dancer is that I didn't think of the administrative side that comes with having an organized business. I was using the honor system when dealing with payments and conditions agreed upon for each event. Thankfully, I've never had a bad experience as a consequence of not having things in writing, but I've heard horror stories of fellow dancers not getting paid for their work. Even though I haven't faced anything this drastic, not having administrative support to back things up led to several inconveniences for me. I was in a vulnerable spot, wondering when and how I would be paid, and sometimes even not knowing certain details of my gig expectations because nothing was specified in writing. Here are three administrative ways to protect yourself when booking gigs independently:

- *Require deposits.* As entertainers, we don't only sacrifice our weekdays, but also weekends and holidays. Some dancers have second jobs that may pay less in a day than a 30-minute set performing does. We often build our schedules around our profession and sometimes have to turn down gigs because we are already booked for another event. A deposit acts as a placeholder on your calendar until the date of the gig. It also guarantees that the client is serious about having you perform. When informed that the deposit becomes nonrefundable days (or even weeks) leading up to their event, they are much less likely to cancel. If they do cancel, at least you can keep their deposit to make up for the other gigs you turned down or any other planning you made to accommodate the event.

- *Use Contracts.* Of course, if you are dancing with an agency, your firm handles this for you. However, if you book gigs independently, a contract is the best way to protect yourself. In this agreement, you can list any expectations you have across the board such as deposit amount & due date payment deadline, etc. I also recommend adding all specific details and special accommodations discussed with the client in the actual contract, itself. That way, if the customer does not make the accommodations agreed to upon showing up to the gig, or if they refuse to pay you because you didn't meet their expectations, you may refer them to the contract they signed, taking legal action if necessary.

- *Consider Performers' Insurance.* A lot of working entertainers do not have liability insurance. However, it is a good idea to think about becoming insured for several reasons. Whether you dance with props or not, there is always a chance something could happen to you or a guest, even if that chance is small. Performers' insurance can protect you against legal claims like guest injury or property damage. Not only that, but once potential customers know that you have liability insurance, you will have a competitive edge over the many performers who do not. Clients often take factors like this into consideration.

Dancer Etiquette

Oriental dance is one of the most misunderstood dance styles out there. Due to this, there are stigmas associated with belly dance that simply aren't true. Over the years of surrounding myself with seasoned professionals and eventually going pro myself, I learned of certain behaviors performers are encouraged and discouraged to partake in as a part of "belly dance etiquette." They are the following:

- **Be professional at all times.** When in doubt, refer to Chapter 8. Professionalism goes a long way in any situation.

- **Keep your character.** Guests look at the belly dancer as more than just dance entertainment. This is the magic behind the whole aura the dancer gives off. Think of the well-known princes & princesses we see at theme parks. They carry themselves a certain way to maintain the "magic" of the character they are portraying. This is the same concept as the belly dancer. When you show up to a gig, you are in character. Many of the other tips listed here will refer back to this.

- **Use proper cover-ups.** At gigs, make sure to cover your costume during breaks and before and after you dance. This can be done with an abaya or kaftan (veils are generally discouraged). It's important to use coverups for multiple reasons. Primarily, your costume is distracting. When you are not performing, exposing yourself in costume will still call attention from patrons. This could even be found as offensive in certain circumstances. Additionally, being exposed in your costume when you aren't in performance mode takes away from the magic of being in character. The belly dancer is ideally seen as enchanting and mysterious. If everyone sees the dancer in costume munching on snacks in the dining area, there is no more novelty or mystery.

- *Wear Shoes.* Unless you are performing at a festival or an event with special accommodations made for barefoot dance, wear shoes. This is especially true for restaurant and hookah lounge gigs. There could be tiny pieces of glass on the floor from broken china or even hot coals from a hookah! You never know what you could step on, so wearing shoes is an important way to protect yourself.

- ***Use appropriate music.*** As belly dancers, we have a wide variety of cultures we work with. Therefore, it's imperative to ask the client their music preferences *before* showing up to that gig. In the past, I've had certain clients request only classical Arabic instrumentals, while other clients gave me free rein to select whichever music I felt was best. With songs in a foreign language, always learn the full translation of what you are dancing to. As educated Oriental dance artists, we must be respectful of the cultures we cater to.

- *Accepting tips.* How belly dancers should and should not accept tips is still widely debated among the belly dance community. A good number of dancers still accept tips in their bras (although this is highly discouraged) while others refuse to accept tips anywhere on their body. From my experience (particularly mistakes early on in my dance career), I've found that accepting tips in one's costume (bra or skirt) can possibly come with sexual connotations in the eyes of patrons. In western countries such as the USA, many guests are unaware of the culture associated with belly dance. The intention of tipping this way may be innocent, but sometimes it can lead to not so innocent gestures that put the dancer at risk. I along with dancers I've studied under, only accept tips in the form of it being handed to me or in the form of a money shower. Tipping this way avoids inappropriate touching, both accidental and intentional. It also teaches uninformed patrons how to respectfully tip you.

- ***Don't undercut.*** As mentioned in Chapter 6, it doesn't only hurt others, but it also hurts yourself in the long run financially.

- ***Avoid staying for dinner afterward.*** In past gigs, I had several situations where the host invited me to eat with the guests after my set. While this gesture is kind and the offer is appreciated, accepting to do so is unprofessional. As a performer, you were booked to do one service—perform! By staying past your agreed time, you now run the risk of transitioning from the professional entertainer to just another informal guest in event attendees' eyes. Not only that, but this once again takes away from the "magic" behind the belly dancer mentioned before. By sitting down to eat with guests, you are no longer the mysterious, enchanting belly dancer. Remember, as an entertainer, you are in character, and breaking it takes away from the performance. It's tough saying no to this common offer, especially when you danced for 30 minutes straight and could use a post-workout meal! However, it's not worth the risk. The best plan of action is to thank them for their courtesy, but you made other plans and must leave immediately after the gig.

- *Avoid romantic encounters with clients or venue owners.* Remember that time when two of your coworkers in the office dated and eventually had major workplace problems because of it? Well, it's the same in the entertainment industry. As a professional belly dancer, performing is your job. It is not leisure. Of course, there are exceptions to every rule. However, mixing business with pleasure can often lead to burned bridges in the long run if the romance ends.

- ***Dealing with propositions.*** It bears repeating that belly dance is misunderstood. Due to the nature of our art, onlookers may apply a sexual connotation to what we do. I, along with others I know, have been propositioned for intimate services more than once. It's not uncommon to be offered hundreds or even thousands of dollars for inappropriate acts. If ever encountered with this proposition, it's imperative to be professional when declining. I say when and not if for a reason. Accepting money for sexual service is prostitution and goes against the standard most Oriental dance artists work hard to uphold. If the proposition is made online, the best plan of action is to ignore the message or block them. When encountering these offers in person, it's recommended to politely inform that you don't do that rather than respond in a rude manner. Even though you may rightfully feel offended, you are still a business and must carry yourself as such.

- *Avoid slander.* Avoid talking down about other dancers in your community. Not only does this come off as unprofessional, but even if it is innocent, or, in your opinion, accurate, it is not a nice thing to do. Supporting each other goes a long way, even if it means respecting each other's differences from a distance.

Expand Your Horizons

Many of us as performance artists become quite comfortable after years of experience. Often, this complacency is to a fault. For a short time, I was in this category. I felt like I knew all I needed to know and was so set in my ways that my dance skills were limited. My style was naturally folkloric and there were certain techniques and props that I took no interest in learning because I felt like I didn't have to. However, I didn't realize that I was restricting the amount of opportunities for gigs because of this. In the past, clients have selected other dance services over mine because they used certain props that I didn't. This was mind-opening and taught me the importance of humility and constantly improving oneself.

Throughout your career as a professional belly dancer, you will learn that it's imperative to constantly expand your horizons, regardless of whether you've been dancing for a couple of years or a couple of decades! There are several ways to broaden your knowledge as a dancer. Workshops at festivals are a great way to gain insight from world-renowned artists and learn new techniques. If you aim to eventually become a teacher, get certified in one or more group/dance fitness programs. Another great way to expand your horizons is by reading about the history of this art form and the cultures surrounding it. Learning other styles of dances are a wonderful way to increase your versatility and also improve your chances of getting booked. Consistent reinvention in your craft is not just important because it increases your opportunity, but it also makes you more rounded as an artist, and that is a satisfying feeling.

Conclusion

As you embark on your journey as a professional belly dance entertainer, take into consideration that every performer's career is different. The topics covered in this book are based on my experiences through trial and error and meant to serve as a guide, although I do encourage every dancer to decide for themselves on what they should do based on their unique circumstances.

In this profession, no two gigs are alike and there are always surprises along the way. Remember that as a working entertainer, you are an artist, as well as a business. Be professional, be resilient, and shimmy on!